I T SEEMS appropriate for the William Alanson White Psychiatric Foundation, in the midst of the Second World War, to republish an essay of Dr. White's about the First.

His thoughts at that time had to do with war and with the nature of the peace to follow, and the kind of world that might emerge.

More than twenty years have passed; the brief illusion of security has vanished; and once again a way of life is locked in death struggle. The same problems with which Dr. White then dealt, again confront us. This crystallization of his thoughts and speculations has a very special significance for us today.

THOUGHTS OF A PSYCHIATRIST ON THE WAR AND AFTER

BY

WILLIAM A. WHITE, M. D.

Supt. of St. Elizabeth's Hospital, Washington, D. C.; Professor
of Nervous and Mental Diseases, Georgetown University;
Professor of Nervous and Mental Diseases,
George Washington University.

NEW YORK
PAUL B. HOEBER
1919

Contents

Introduction

PSYCHIATRY as a medical specialty, devoted to the treatment of mental diseases, has for generations been considered under the limiting concept insanity. Recent years have seen its evolution from this limitation to include minor degrees of illness recognized as imbalances of the personality make-up and included in various disorders of adaptation classified as the neuroses and psycho-neuroses. A more intimate study of these conditions has resulted in the recognition that all such disorders were defects in the capacity for adjustment, and these defects have come to be more and more recognized as defects in adjustment to the social environment. Human psychology has found itself sorely limited when it confined its study solely to man as an individual, and has come into its true place and possibilities only when it has learned to consider man as a social animal. Society, while it is composed of individuals, reflects its degree of development in each individual psyche, so that man and society occupy relations of mutual interdependence, each profoundly affecting the other. In his efforts to aid the sick individual the psychiatrist thus comes to consider of necessity the social values that are reflected in the personality before him.

In these serious days of social upheaval the psychiatrist has been confronted by an exceptional material of mental disorders of adjustment, not only in the soldier population faced with the possibility of being called upon to make the ultimate renunciation, but in the civilian population as well, torn by all the anxieties of having loved ones at the front and by the necessities of the radical rearrangement of their lives in innumerable ways at home. The psychiatrist has, as a result, been confronted with huge problems of large numbers of individuals to treat and the further task of attempting to fit all sorts of unusual types of personality into some sort of social usefulness. Out of these experiences it is natural that the meaning of the present conflict and the readjustments necessary to bring it to a successful issue and to carry over success into the period of readjustment should have been a matter for serious thought. All about us new concepts are being born as old concepts are being given new meanings by the events of the day, and the symbols which are used to indicate them are being reënergized. Patriotism has come to have a broader and a deeper meaning which is making for an extension of ideals and aims beyond geographical boundaries, and thus is motivating new forms of conduct. The psychological principles underlying these changes are, as they appear to the author, briefly set down in these "thoughts."

WILLIAM A. WHITE.

The Social Perspective

CHAPTER I

I N THESE days, when the militant upheaval of the world seems to be knocking the props from under all of the established conditions which had come to be looked upon, thought about, felt, and wished as stable, it would seem to be worth while to try—even though it be in a small and perhaps, in some directions, an uninformed way—to trace in the events that are rapidly occurring the operation of laws and principles which in the end will make for evolution, for progress, for development, and for better conditions of living, in order that we may the more intelligently go forward with the times in a feeling of sympathetic coöperation with that undying hope in those aspirational values that we have always felt somehow controlled the order of things. The immense complexity of the conditions involved makes, it seems to me, a survey from every point of view of some possible value in the hope that some common ground may be reached by approaching the problems from all angles. The uniformity of natural laws has made me feel that perhaps as a psychiatrist, who is constantly faced with the problem of regulating individual lives, the point of view developed in this work might be of service in outlining principles which would be applicable to the larger problems of society.

Because of the tremendous extent of the present conflict, and only for that reason, it seems to me, are we inclined to view with alarm the ultimate resolution of the present state of affairs. Such upheavals have always been with us in the smaller problems of the parts of the social organism. Individuals have always had the tragedy of frustrated lives to face with the necessity for radical readjustment or complete failure as the alternatives; social groups and even nations have had the same problems to meet, but never before has the whole world been so put to it. It is the scale on which the present situation is drawn that destroys our perspective rather than the nature of the problems that are involved and which, therefore, because we cannot escape a personal reckoning with the results, suffuses the whole situation with that feeling of anxiety which grips in the face of overwhelming forces that push us irresistibly into the very midst of the great unknown. But mankind has not changed over-night, and it must be that we can observe, if we but look with seeing eyes, the same instincts, the same tendencies that we have all along been familiar with as we have watched man struggle with his problems elsewhere, writ so large perhaps as, by that very token, to be out of the field of our clear vision, so big, so in evidence that we fail, for that very reason, to see them. It is reminiscent of that game of our childhood when we hid an object by putting it in the most conspicuous place in the room.

All this is not to say that we are not on the eve of momentous and far-reaching changes, but the beginnings of these very changes have for years been taking root all about us and reach in their origins to those instinctive springs of human conduct that we are already familiar with in other relations. It is rather, I apprehend, here as elsewhere, the desire not to see rather than the fact that there is nothing to see that makes us blind.

The Psychology of Conflict: The Individual Versus the Group

CHAPTER II

THERE are everywhere small groups of pacifists who decry war, who do not believe in fighting, but who do believe in the possibility of a peaceful settlement of all difficulties. But so far as we know, fighting has been one of man's universal ways of reacting ever since he has been upon the earth, and this is true not only of man, but of all animate creation, so long as our concept of fighting is not war alone. Conflict is universal in some form or other, and not only is it not possible to avoid it, but it lies at the very basis of the manifestations of life itself. What do I mean by such a statement?

In so far as life consists in the adaptation of the living being to its environment it involves a continuous overcoming of resistances, from the painstaking carrying of each grain of dirt by the ant as it tunnels out its nest to the molding of clay and iron into the brick and steel framework of a great building; and the evolution of life to higher forms implies an ever-increasing capacity for better and better, that is, finer adjustments. Life is always at war with the elements, and is destroyed by too much heat on the one hand or too little on the other, by too much water or too little, in short by the very elements themselves upon which life depends if the adjustment falls outside certain limits. Life in its myriad forms has to adjust itself to all the varying conditions of environment, and somehow struggles through all the sturdier for the hardships suffered. The "survival of the fit" means that only those who are able to weather the storm are able to live. Nature acts like a careful breeder, throwing out all stock that is inferior, that is incapable of surviving the hardships inflicted by a given set of selective agents— heat, cold, dryness, moisture, high altitude, special enemies, etc. And when it comes to man we know that a young man's future is by no means assured by removing the obstacles from his path, rather the contrary. Character is developed by overcoming obstacles, not by going around them.

But it is not this struggle with the environment that I wish to emphasize, important as it may be. It is the struggle within which is of supreme significance— the struggle of man with himself, the old, old struggle which has been emphasized over and over again by religion and by the poet and the artist. It is the struggle of man, ever on the upward path from savagery to civilization and then to an ever better civilization. This is the struggle which, it seems to me, must be understood if we are to understand war.[1]

[1] In order that the nature of this inner conflict may be understood it will be helpful to refer to certain historical facts in the growth of the science of psychology.

Psychology, until about a generation ago, was largely tinged with metaphysical speculation. It was based upon the results of introspective examination rather than upon the results of objective observation which had come to be the method of the other natural sciences. It was among the last of the sciences to adopt the method of experimental verification and to take its place in the laboratory along with the rest of them. When it did, however, finally evolve to the laboratory stage it occupied itself with experimental refinements. Vision was examined to define its range, not only in terms of distance, but of lateral extent; the visibility of the cardinal colors was examined in the same way and then the range of color vision itself, that is, the number of color tones that were distinguishable; the degrees of brightness were arranged in a scale in a similar way; and the rapidity, measured in hundredths of a second, with which the observer could respond to the several visual stimuli was recorded. The other sense organs were examined in like manner and laws were evolved based upon the nature of series of least observable differences in stimuli. Psychology, in this state of its development, was in reality only a refined physiology of the sense organs, defining their capacities for reaction in more definite terms of time and space and of the physical characteristics of the stimulus.

For this psychology, which was a refined physiology, the sensation was the irreducible unit out of

The human animal, like all animals, has certain fundamental instincts which it spends its life in endeavoring to satisfy. Just what these are, how they are to be classified, is a matter of considerable difference of opinion, but they include the hunger instinct, the sex instinct, the instinct to fight enemies, the instinct to seek safety, the parental instinct and the instinct of gregariousness. The parental instinct might, perhaps, be classified as a development of the sex instinct on the one hand and the instinct of self-preservation on the other, in which the result of satisfying the sex hunger—the child—is desired both as a means of security in old age and also as a means of projecting one's self into the future, the instinct for immortality. All of the instincts may be classified into two fundamental ones, namely, the self-preservation instinct (type hunger), and the race-preservation instinct (type sexuality). Or from another point of view, the attitude of the individual towards the object of instinct, into acquisitive tendencies, the effort to acquire the object (type love) and avertive tendencies, the effort to destroy or avoid the object (type hate, subtypes anger and fear).

These instincts in their primitive manifestations condition the ways of reacting of the lower animals which make up behavior. They cause all of those more or less complicated series of activities that produce the phenomena of mating and all those subsidiary activities including the care of the young, and those other activities that have to do with attacking and

---

which all that was mental was built up. If I, for example, see a book lying on the table before me, this experience can be analyzed into its component sensory units. The color of the book, lighter where the light strikes it, darker in shadow, is analyzable into its component sensory qualities; the perception of its distance is dependent upon sensations (unconscious) of the stress and strain of the eye muscles as they move the two eyes into a position which brings the book into clear vision, into focus; the perception of the object as a book is again dependent, not upon immediate sensations, but upon a combination, an association of these with remembered groups of similar sensations, which groups, occurring over and over again in the course of our lives, have, with the aid of memory associations, gradually built up the concept book: the perception of the roughness or smoothness, as the case may be, of the cover is also but sensational material, but here again, largely inferred from the past touch experiences rather than dependent upon present sensations. The sensation is the unit out of which consciousness is built up by a progressive series of combinations into percepts, concepts, abstract ideas.

This is a workable method of studying certain mental processes so long as we are dealing with subjects that can be interrogated, but for studying the mind in its manifestations in animals other than man it is impracticable. Here a method of objective observation becomes necessary, and accordingly the animal psychologists had to build up a science from which introspection, which had so long remained the keynote to all things psychological, was completely eliminated. The necessity for the elimination of introspection resulted in refinements of method which shortly came to be applied to the study of human psychology. The refined physiology of the sense organs gave way to a study of the observable conduct of the individual by the new school of "behaviorists."

The behaviorists no longer asked such questions as, What is the least increase in the strength of a stimulus that is perceivable? but, What is the individual doing? This was a much more pertinent question for psychology to answer, for it is a question which must be answered in terms of the whole individual and therefore in terms that are truly psychological, while the earlier form of question, because it could only be answered in terms of the function of a particular part of the individual (an organ, such as the eye), is for that very reason, answerable in terms which are clearly physiological. For example, a man leaves his house, walks down town, stops at a real estate broker's, signs certain papers, gives a check and receives a deed in return. The answer to What is the man doing? would be that He is buying a house. If all of the observable data are present the question can be answered, some behaviorists say, without reference at all to the data of introspection. However, there can be no question but that psychology had made a great advance when it came to deal with conduct, in fact it, for the first time, was primarily interested in material that was truly psychological.

It remained for the psychoanalyst to take the next step which, while it continued to deal with conduct, did not ignore the introspective data. He saw the importance of recognizing that the mind was an expression of the individual as a whole and that in the field of the psyche were fought out those battles of the instincts each of which tried to capture the individual and bend all of his energies to its purpose. Conduct thus becomes the final result in action of the various instinctive tendencies as they struggle for ascendency and succeed, fail, or more frequently reach some compromise.

In this struggle of the instinctive tendencies, this constant "battle of motives," each tendency fights, so to speak, to bring to pass the realization of its own particular trend, it seeks certain ends, it tries to compass them, it desires to bring them about, in short it wishes for certain results. The "battle of motives" for the control of the individual thus becomes a battle of wishes and that motive or that wish succeeds which is the stronger. The individual does what, in the last analysis, he wanted to do. In terms of conduct the man bought a house, but if we also take into account the data of introspection we find in addition that he wanted to buy a house in the country which he could look forward to as a home when he retired from business. The wish has replaced the sensation as the ultimate psychological unit.

The replacement of the sensation by the wish as the unit of mental life has not only been of momentous importance from a purely scientific standpoint, but it has had the effect of humanizing the science of mind. Psychology can no longer be content to deal with abstract scientific concepts, but it must deal with actual, living human material, with men as they are, with their aspirations and disappointments, their hopes, their fears, their loves and hates. Psychology has become humanized. (See Holt, Edward B.: "The Freudian Wish and Its Place in Ethics." New York, 1915.)

overcoming other animals either for food or as enemies, and the means of escape, flight, etc., from enemies of overwhelming strength.

The progress of mankind from savagery to civilization does not consist in the destruction of these instincts, but in the suppression—repression—of the primitive ways of satisfying them and the utilization of the energies so repressed to find satisfaction in ways that are progressively more and more removed from the primitive types. This is the process of sublimation. What are the forces that bring about this change?

The force which deflects the primitive instincts of love and hate from immediate satisfaction by at once acquiring the loved object or destroying the hated enemy, is that group of necessities which arise as a consequence of man's living together in groups, the so-called instinct of gregariousness, or the herd instinct. So long as one animal could stand alone it not only might satisfy its instincts to mate and to kill, but it was to its distinct advantage to do so, for only by so doing could it insure its own existence and the continued existence of the species. When, however, as with man, it became evident that for purposes of protection from superior enemies it was desirable to herd in bands, there arose the factor of the welfare of the group as a distinct end in itself, often if not always, of superior importance to the welfare of the individual members. To kill a member of the group, for example, tended to weaken the strength of that group and, by the same token, to make it less effective as a protective device for the individual members, the one who did the killing as well as the others. Therefore there arose a situation in which the interests of the individual and the interests of the herd were not the same, they were opposed and in consequence the group being more powerful than any individual member of it, the interests of the individual had to give way to those of the group. Killing, therefore, had to be done only with the consent of the herd when it felt that its interests as a group demanded it. Individual feuds tended to give place

to the more orderly procedure of trial and condemnation. The instinct to kill was therefore sidetracked into a more devious path for its satisfaction, a path beset with all sorts of obstacles from the standpoint of the individual's cravings, but one which served the interests of the herd far better. The instinct, from being satisfied by actual killing, came to seek satisfaction in the sublimated forms of condemnation, trial, etc., and if perhaps the criminal were acquitted it failed by so much in attaining its goal. It is the same with the acquiring of food. The interests of the herd—society—demand that food shall be acquired as a result of work; work is paid for with money, and the money in turn may be exchanged for food. The interesting point here is that the work shall be of a character to benefit the herd, it must be socially acceptable, a socially useful form of work.

Here, then, in this opposition of the interests of the individual in his efforts to satisfy his fundamental instincts and the interests of the herd, is a basic problem upon the successful solution of which depends the success of man's efforts to reach ever higher goals in his struggle upwards. This is the fundamental conflict which conditions man's activities as a member of society. What is the method of its solution?

In the process of evolution organisms have developed of ever-increasing complexity in correspondence with an equally increasing nicety of adaptation to the complexities of their environment. This has meant, among other things, that no single function or organ of the entire organism has evolved to the exclusion of the other functions or organs; each has developed, but in subservience to the needs of the whole. Organisms have not developed that were all digestive apparatus or all brain, or all liver or kidney or other organ. Each organ, while developing, had had its functional growth fitted into the needs of the whole. The digestive apparatus needs a brain to direct the finding and appropriating of proper food, the brain needs a digestive apparatus to furnish it nourishment, and both need adequate excretory organs to prevent the waste products which accumulate from clogging their delicately adjusted mechanisms. This process of developing the parts in the service of the whole is the process of integration.

The process of integration applies equally to the instincts which, after all, may be reduced to efforts towards the satisfaction of organic needs; the hunger instinct is primarily the effort of the stomach to satisfy its cravings; the instinct to fight is the effort of the so-called kinetic system, of which the muscles are obviously the most important part, to gain satisfaction in safety by the destruction of a dangerous enemy, and so forth. Now the well-rounded, integrated individual is one in whom all of the instincts operate, but in the service of the needs of the whole individual. Thus we eat when we need food, we fight when fighting is necessary to eliminate the danger from an enemy threatening destruction, and so with the rest.

When, for example, any one instinct is enabled, for any reason, to gain the mastery of the whole organism so that it dominates its activities, that individual is sick. The dominance of the hunger instinct makes the glutton, of the sexual instinct the Don Juan, of the acquisitive instinct the miser or the thief, and he is sick because the instinct domination from which he suffers has resulted in activities which are not useful to the herd. He becomes asocial or antisocial, according as to whether his activities are negatively or positively injurious to the herd.

It is the same with the social organism. It is made up of many different groups each engaged in its own peculiar activities, doctors, lawyers, mechanics, soldiers, engineers, clergymen, laborers, farmers, artists, etc. Now if any one of these groups should come to dominate the activities of the whole social organism, it too would be sick. Society needs all of their activities, but it needs them, as the body needs its organs, subordinated to the needs of the whole. Farmers are needed to produce the food, railroad operatives are needed to transport it, doctors to care for the sick and prevent disease, lawyers to assist the administration of justice, clergymen to minister to the spiritual needs. It is only when all work together for the common good of the whole that the society is adequately integrated and so healthy. If, for example, the shoemakers should dominate, then every one would be at the job of making shoes without thought of the necessity for getting food or the administration of those necessary laws upon which all cooperation must depend. Such a society would be manifestly sick, but, too, it would of necessity soon cease to exist.

An exceedingly important aspect of this process of integration, and one which it is necessary to bear in mind, is that integration is in itself a process of development, and failure of integration is, therefore, an indication of lack of development or of relative immaturity. This is, of course, only another way of saying that the domination of any particular instinct is detrimental to the social usefulness of the individual and therefore tends to unfit that individual for the fullest life as a member of the social group.

The failure of integration, the domination of particular instinctive trends, inasmuch as it renders the individual asocial or antisocial, thus brings to bear the operation of the herd critique directed against such individuals and such activities as are so conditioned. The operation of this herd critique seems therefore to force the individual along lines of activity which shall be socially useful. It represents the force of the herd making for its own ends and compelling the individual to abandon—repress—the immediate gratification of his own instincts and the utilization of the energies thus turned aside in sublimated forms of activity which shall be useful to the herd. To put it another way: The force which, in its negative aspect makes for repression—the herd critique—produces in its positive aspect the desire for the reward of social esteem.

This double negative and positive aspect of the herd critique is characteristic of all progressive tendencies. They are first repressed and only later become the objects of desire in a sublimated form. We repress those instinctive cravings which lie near to the surface, which we are only a little distance from really wanting to yield to. After having developed a firm sublimation, however, we can allow our instincts fuller play. Love may thus literally replace hate. For example, the savage kills with relatively little repugnance, but as society develops the instinct of overcoming our enemy in the primitive and final way has to be repressed for the common good. Later, however, the work of killing becomes a highly exalted profession in the soldier when it is elevated to an end higher than the satisfaction of an individual hatred, namely the end of the saving of the group—nation—from destruction by another group. Similarly, but more subtly, the instinct to build as expressed by the child playing in mud and dirt has later to be repressed, because it becomes obnoxious to the grown-ups, but in the course of development the child who expressed this early interest in building may find satisfaction in progressively more acceptable ways and means and become an engineer or architect. His instinct has remained the same but it is applied in more socially acceptable and useful ways, it has become sublimated. It is, therefore, not the instinct that changes, but its application. Development might thus be expressed by a description of the objects of interest as they successively replace one another and represent progressively more socially valuable activities.

The same method of reasoning can be applied to the social group, and we recognize development in this larger aspect as based upon the nature of the objects which social groups seek to attain. The essentially imperialistic group that is bent upon conquering weaker groups and using them as sources of revenue, slaves either in the primitive physical sense of that term or the more developed economic sense, is admittedly lower in the scale of social development than the society that exercises a protecting function over weaker groups and helps them develop along the lines of their natural tendencies.

A most important aspect for an understanding of mechanisms of repression and sublimation is the way in which we project ourselves into these various situations. This, for reasons that will appear, is not, however, obvious. For example the perpetrator of a grave social offense is hated. The obvious reason for our hate is that the offense brings misery and suffering to others. Looked into a little more carefully, the hate can be seen to have self-protective aspects, The criminal's act is calculated to destroy the existing order of things, and unless it is put down vigorously, the criminal apprehended and punished, that is, confined against further similar activities, we ourselves may suffer from its activities. And punishment is rationalized largely by the belief that it will be deterrent to others who may be similarly tempted, despite the fact that actual experience by no means shows that prevention of crime is proportionate to severity of punishment. Further than this the temptations to which the criminal yielded are vaguely—unconsciously—apprehended as of a character to tempt us, and so in hating the criminal we are really bringing to bear the so-called antipathic emotions, our avertive tendencies, upon those tendencies which we unconsciously recognize within ourselves and so forcing, so to speak, ourselves along the upward path of development away from socially destructive forms of conduct which would tend to disintegrate that very social organization upon which we so much depend for opportunities to realize the best that is in us. This projection of ourselves into such a situation is therefore but a symbolization of our own inner conflict between our ideals and our instinctive tendencies as they are seen in operation in the conflict between, in this instance, the criminal and society.[2]

To elaborate this thesis a little further from the point of view of the relatively undeveloped, infantile, character of unsocial activities: The child of two or three years that appropriates something that does not belong to it is not treated either as a criminal or with hate. It is corrected,

[2] I have elaborated this point of view in the chapter on the criminal in my book "The Principles of Mental Hygiene," published by the Macmillan Company, New York, 1917.

often in a more or less facetious way, to the end of bringing it to understand the differences between mine and thine. Our attitude, while one of repression, is also one of education and emotionally is kindly and indulgent. Toward the criminal, on the other hand, it is one of repression, punishment, and hate. Why the difference? It is because in the child's activities we recognize something that belongs to the child period, while in the criminal we see a form of activity which should have been left behind in the process of growth and development, should have become a part of the individual's past. We see the anachronism of an infantile type of conduct in an adult setting and as such stamp it as wrong, as unnatural, because it does not conform to the normal, that is, the usual. Similarly with other forms of abnormal conduct. We are coming to see in all of them ways of expressing the instincts which are relatively undeveloped, infantile. Among the so-called "insane" the examples are without number. In the mentally ill patient who has to be cared for as a child we see an individual who has returned to certain infantile ways of reacting by a process known as regression. We may be disgusted with such a reaction, but we are indulgent and helpful on the theory that the patient is ill. Such conduct does not call for hate, because it is only calculated to injure the sick individual; it is only passively, so to speak, antisocial and not actively and aggressively antisocial as in the case of the so-called criminal.[3]

To put it somewhat differently, the herd critique is directed against antisocial types of conduct, and antisocial types of conduct are types which are relatively infantile types and anachronisms because occurring in an adult setting. The object of the critique is to press the activities of the individual into channels that lead to conduct useful to the herd and so is, after all, a form of projected critique against those tendencies in ourselves which would lead us into forms of conduct essentially selfish. This sort of repressive mechanism

is necessary because we all have the same instinctive cravings and only differ as we learn to get satisfaction from those objects and forms of activity which are socially useful, that is, when we get away from the necessity for the immediate satisfaction of those cravings in primitive and concrete ways; until, in other words, we have learned to sublimate.

One more important principle can be illustrated by a further analogy between society and the living organism. What the organism does to neutralize its cravings and to relate itself to its environment is a function either of some organ or of the organism as a whole. When the function becomes efficient and is maintained for a considerable period of time there results a structure which is laid down to carry on the function. The function of the circulation of nutrient fluids in the lower monocellular organisms is carried on in a seemingly haphazard sort of way, the fluid flowing here and there throughout the cell in no previously laid-out channels. In the higher organisms there has been developed a circulatory system which fulfills this function in a very efficient way. This laying down of structure to fulfill function I have called the structuralization of function, and it is one of the prominent characteristics in the evolution of organisms. Thus the circulatory system may be said to be the solution, in structure, of the problem of getting the nutrient fluids to the different parts of the organism. From the same point of view the lungs are the organism's solution of the problem of utilizing oxygen, the gastrointestinal tract the solution of the problem of utilizing proteins, starches, and fats, the liver the solution of the problem of using sugar, etc.

Similarly in society. Railroads represent in part the circulatory system, which is society's solution of the problem of transportation, which is so crudely carried out in primitive communities; the groups of tailors and cloth makers represent society's solution of the problem of supplying clothes, etc.[4]

---

[3] For a further discussion of mental illness as asocial and criminal conduct as antisocial see my "Principles of Mental Hygiene."

[4] For a further discussion of the principles underlying integration and the place of the psyche in development see my article "The Significance for

These various solutions serve their several purposes so long as no great demands are made upon them different from those which called them into being. For example, the kidneys work very efficiently until called upon to excrete substances for which their efficiency was never developed, as, for example, alcohol or corrosive sublimate. Analogously certain social groups break in an attempt to adjust to conditions which they have never been developed to meet. The hand weavers suffered great hardship as a result of the introduction of machinery to do the work which they had learned to do by hand. The readjustment threw large numbers out of work and into great want and privation. A new type of worker had to be developed to meet the new conditions. In the development and evolution of organisms the history of organs is quite similar; for example, the substitution of lungs for gills when animals left their watery habitat and became terrestrial.

The significant facts are that new structures arise to meet new conditions and that the old structures have to be discarded, destroyed. The greater the demand for readjustment the more extensive the destruction. It is as if development went on in a certain direction as far as it could go and then, because the limit had been reached in that particular direction, what had already been developed must be destroyed and a new start made towards a different objective. In this process not infrequently the race or the species comes

Psychotherapy of Child's Developmental Gradients and the Dynamic Differentiation of the Head Region," *Psychoanalyt. Rev., V,* January, 1918.

to an end because it is incapable of sustaining itself during the period of readjustment. Development has as one of its aspects destruction—disintegration of all that stands in the way. In the moral sphere we call it renunciation. The alcoholic must renounce alcohol if he wishes to become socially rehabilitated.

I have devoted so much space to the setting forth of certain principles of human behavior and drawing analogies between the living organism and society because it seems to be essential to have this larger viewpoint in order to approach the problem of war in a judicial, unprejudiced frame of mind. The state of mind produced by war is so laden with the emotion of hate that our vision is likely to be restricted within the limits of that emotion and so fail us in acquiring that broader outlook which I believe so essential in dealing with all things human. Then again we are still inclined to be immature in our judgments of others, to see them only in terms of individuals like ourselves, and so fail utterly in evaluating characters which have grown up and developed in response to conditions different from those with which we are familar. For this reason alone whole races, with us—for example, the Orientals—remain everlasting mysteries. We must learn to see individuals, races, species as but reactions of adaptation, more or less successfully integrated, to meet the problems which have confronted in them the unfolding of the great creative energy in the face of the obstacles which have blocked their pathways.

The Integration of Social Groups—Culture

CHAPTER III

W E ARE now in a position to consider some of the special psychological problems presented by war. We shall find, among other things, that a very important distinction must be made as to whether we view the phenomena from the standpoint of the individual or from that of the group to which he belongs.

I have stressed the analogies between the living organism and society. The evolution of the living organism has been along the lines of the development of organs which are structures laid down to answer demands made upon the capacity for functional adaptation. In the same way society, by the process of the specialization of activities by separate groups, has responded to the demands made upon it in a quite similar way. And further, just as in the evolution of life organisms have become more complex in the sense that their several parts were more and more specialized for particular functions—that is, they developed more organs—so societies have become more and more complex and have come to include a greater and greater number of specialized groups. In both the living organism and in society the progressively increasing number of organs are able to function effectively because they have been integrated, that is, their several functions have been so related that, while they each serve their own special ends, their activities are subordinated to the good of the whole group, thus bringing about a hierarchy of organs which represent structuralized functions.

Among interrelated social groups each group has an end which is purely individual and another end which is directed to the good of the larger group of which it is a component part, and so on if this larger group is a member of a still larger one. From the standpoint of each group, therefore, there are two fundamental interests, namely the interests of the individual member of the group (be it the individual as such or a social group within a nation, or a nation within a league of nations) and the interests of the group as a whole. As already explained, these two lines of interest frequently intersect. It obviously depends, therefore, to a great extent from which point of view, the individual or the group, a given action is observed whether it will be considered a desirable form of activity or otherwise. This fact is of prime importance in considering social activities as they are expressed either in the conduct of the individual or the acts of a nation. For example killing is a crime when committed by a person in his individual capacity, unless, of course, in self-defense, but when committed by a soldier it is highly commended for the reason that in his capacity as soldier he is acting for the group, serving its interests. This distinction between individual and group has, too, to be further modified on the basis of the point in development which each has attained in the general scheme of evolution. The conflict between the interests of the individual and those of the group, the eternal desire of the individual to find the fulfillment of his inner needs, the recognition that they can only be adequately fulfilled through and not in opposition to the group, the needs of the group and the necessity for forcing the individual to bring them to pass, are the conflicting, crossing, and supplementary lines of force that make for the final results. Just as multicellularity was a necessary precondition to specialization of cells so that each could best realize its own possibilities and develop function to the highest point of refinement, so society is a necessary precondition to the highest development of the individual and the fullest utilization of his powers.

I have also stressed the process of integration in the description of the development of organs and groups and their relations to one another with the corresponding subordination of their respective individual ends to the good of the larger whole. It therefore follows in general that the older organs and groups have solved their respective problems up to a certain point better than the younger ones, and are thus more capable of functioning efficiently, of course on the assumption that they have not come to the end of their capacity for readjustment and are therefore fixed. The heart has solved the problem of propelling the blood and done it so effectively that its structure is capable of very little modification and also susceptible of relatively little variation in functional capacity or modification at the behest of other organs, for example the lungs. So with old social structures such as the medieval trade guilds, which were relatively stable. Stability is a desirable end, inasmuch as it makes for efficiency within the limits of its capacity for adaptation, but undesirable in the face of necessities for radical readjustments just because of those limits.

Conduct, therefore, has to be judged from the point of view of the relative maturity or immaturity of the reacting individual, organ, or group. For the savage there is one standard of conduct, a primitive one; for the civilized individual another and much higher standard is the measure. So for certain nations that are as yet in a relatively immature stage of civilization the standard is much different from that of more developed, higher evolved nations. And again nations may have evolved to a point which demands higher types of individual and social conduct, but it does not follow that when such nations attempt to unite their efforts into a larger group, a league of nations, the standard will remain as high. Quite the contrary. The higher integration is in a youthful, infantile, primitive undeveloped, immature state and so, even though the constituent nations are highly evolved their group actions may take on the char-

acteristics which we have learned to associate with a relatively immature state of development. Lying and deceit of all kinds are pretty well tabooed as types of individual reaction, but they are still in evidence in the diplomatic inter-relations between nations. International relations are higher forms of reality situations which have not yet developed mature and efficient types of reaction which have been laid down in an enduring structure of custom and law. The several political units look upon each other as natural enemies and seek to overcome each other by relatively immature, primitive, unsublimated methods. Nations in their international relations have then to repeat the story of evolution much as does each child from the moment of impregnation to adulthood. The individual members of the race, however, are already highly evolved as individuals, and in this new process of integration are called upon to make adjustments relatively of an immature kind. This necessity for going backward on the path of adjustment has been variously called reversion, regression, and dedifferentiation. It involves a casting aside of already acquired adjustments and reverting to an historically earlier type which had been found useful in the past experiences of the individual or the race. In evaluating human conduct during a period of war, therefore, a distinction has to be made between conduct which is representative of the level already attained by the individual and the level of the race in its newest efforts.

The apparently new phenomena which seem to have been added during a state of war are these phenomena of regression, and they are apparently new because we see them become manifest in persons who, as individuals, had always maintained a high standard of personal conduct, but in the new conditions imposed by war become violent partisans from whom reason seems temporarily to have vanished and who, contrary to everything in their past history, become apologists for every kind of regressive tendency.

Such manifestations surprise because we had come to think that they were impossible, in other words we have thought that the ground gained by culture was gained for all time and so we are always unprepared to see such gross lapses. Our belief that all that has been gained by culture will be held is after all nothing but a wish, and it is because it is a wish, because the belief has back of it the motive power of a wish, that we are so unprepared to find that it is not true, and this despite the fact that we are surrounded by evidences of its untruth all the time. That enormous group of the dependent, defective, and delinquent classes testify in each individual member to the actual fact of regression to earlier cultural levels of reaction.

This matter of regression is one of the most important psychological mechanisms to understand if we are to have any real comprehension of man's cultural advances and set-backs. I have already indicated how each organic need tends to reach satisfaction, but how a conflict arises the net result of which is to press all such needs into the service of the larger whole, be that individual or group. This outer compulsion to serve the larger end can only be successful at the expense of pressing back, repressing, certain components of the energy representing those organic needs which are not addressed to this larger purpose, but, on the contrary, which are addressed to finding immediate, concrete, and selfish satisfaction. Such energies can thereafter only be effectively expended, in a way satisfactory to both the individual and the group ends, in a sublimated form, which means that immediate, concrete, selfish satisfaction must be replaced by a more remote, less concrete, and relatively unselfish type of reaction. The criminal, for example, wants something—money—and proceeds to take it. This is a primitive, immediate, concrete, selfish way of gratifying his wish. The more highly developed man goes by a much more devious path to the goal. He works and earns the money. Perhaps he studies for years to fit himself for the work. He spends weeks, months, perhaps years in slowly accumulating as much money as the thief takes in an hour. And the work that he does is socially useful, it is constructive. For example, he may be a machinist, a builder, a tradesman, or any one of a thousand things which serve

society. He gains the gratification of his wishes in ways that are relatively highly evolved, that yield less immediate satisfaction and substitute a goal to be attained at some future time, that are less concrete—because for the actual money, for example, a way of living is largely substituted—and which are less selfish because the activities which are calculated to earn the money are useful to the social group of which he is a member.

From these illustrations it must be evident that repression is an essential feature in cultural progress. What is not quite so evident, however, is that the repressed material is essentially of the same character in all of us. We have all traveled the same path of development, all started with the same instinctive needs, all been subjected to the same repressive forces. To be sure all persons are not alike; they exhibit differences of character just as they exhibit differences of other sorts, for example, differences of feature. But it is with character as it is with the features, the similarities are much more in evidence than the differences. It is true that no two people look exactly alike, but it is also true that all have two eyes, a nose, and a mouth. The variations must be rung on this substantial background of similarities. That it is so with character we can easily believe when we realize that the human species is five hundred thousands of years old. With such a past shared in common the differences must be relatively very small. The repressed material goes to form what is known as the unconscious, that is, that region of the mind which makes up its past history but of which we are not in ourselves aware.[5]

Inasmuch as the repressed material— the unconscious—is the same, to all intents and purposes, in all of us, it might be well to inquire briefly of what it consists, for we would expect, if this is true, to find that it was such material that invariably came to the surface in states of regression.

The essential nature of the unconscious can be summed up in the single word self-

---

[5] For a discussion of the basic elements of character see my "Mechanisms of Character Formation." Published by The Macmillan Company, New York, 1916.

ish, or self-seeking. It knows only its own individual interests and would go directly to its goal irrespective of anything else. Other individuals' inconvenience, suffering, or even death are of no account to it. Immediate satisfaction of desire by the means most readily available is its only formula, the seeking of pleasure and the avoiding of pain its only object. The unconscious, therefore, contains the records of our past as we have painfully climbed the road to civilization. It contains those tendencies to gluttony, to lust, to lie and deceive, to hate, cruelty, and murder which characterize the savage and the child,[6] and upon the sublimation of which the progress of civilization depends.

---

[6] This may seem a rather extreme statement with regard to the child, but unbiased observation dis-

But this inventory of the unconscious discloses precisely those characteristics which we find coming to the front in wartime and which, when exhibited by persons we have learned to respect, so much surprise us. The explanation is evident. That great region of our past which we all hold in common has been uncovered and instinctive tendencies which had been repressed now again come to the surface and call for satisfaction. It is the phenomenon of regression. The psychic energy, instead of flowing to outside interests, turns back and refloods the channels along which it flowed in the process of development.

---

closes the child as essentially selfish, although the extreme manifestations of this selfishness are commonly held in check. In the child criminal, however, they come to the fore.

Psychological Effects of War

CHAPTER IV

THE phenomena of regression, the failure of sublimation, take on similar characters in the individual and thus also in the group which reflects the conjoined reactions of its individual members. I have already indicated in a general way the nature of some of these reactions, the primitive ones of hate, cruelty, and deceit. In the individuals these tendencies manifest themselves in killing, looting, burning, rape, and all manner of bloodshed and violence, such as bring about the general feeling of the collapse of civilization. Some of these reactions show with especial clearness the regressive tendencies. It is the sex instinct, for example, which, in the course of cultural development, is most subjected to repression and suffers infinite distortions in its efforts to find expression and free itself from the fetters of innumerable taboos. Quite characteristically, therefore, do we find that acts of sexual violence and lawlessness characterize the conduct of the unrestrained soldiery. The sex instinct in its manifold manifestations which under repression produces in times of peace, for the most part, neuroses which are crippling to the individual only, in times of war leads to overt acts of concrete indulgence often at the expense of the lives of others. Loosed from the usual bonds of convention and social restraint it tends to outcrop in veritable orgies of lust.

It is quite similar with other socially repressed tendencies. Hate manifests itself in wanton destruction, an infantile type of reaction, that reminds us of the angered child that breaks up its toys and tears up its books. Some of these hate reactions show peculiarly their infantile sources, such as the defilement of temporary quarters in captured towns, even of the religious utensils and paraphernalia of churches. This latter is a direct manifestation of the infantile reaction of antagonism to authority, secular or spiritual, which marks the course of the emancipation of the child from parental domination. It has at once the meaning of the overthrow of authority and thus the enhancement and dominance of the personal ego and that other primitive characteristic of overcoming an enemy by destroying a symbol of that enemy. This is in accord with the primitive and childlike faith in magic based upon a belief in the omnipotence of thought. If one only thinks a thing hard enough it must be true. Savages use such methods to destroy a foe when they resort to charms and incantations. We do the same in our resort to prayer and especially to lurid posters representing the annihilation of the foe. Similar principles underlie the violent assertion of what we will do and insist upon, of perfervid statements setting forth our invincibility and the sanctity of our purposes as opposed to the ultimate necessity of surrender by the enemy and his essentially selfish and criminal purposes. All such statements seem to gain strength and acceptance, not in proportion to their innate reasonableness, but in proportion to the emphasis with which they are enunciated. Reason seems to have been temporarily dethroned and pure feeling, emotion, takes its place as the motive force of conduct. The wish becomes truly the father to the thought. The long battle for the control of the emotions, of instinct, by the intelligence, seems to have been lost and man slips back to be again dominated by his feelings.

Trotter analyzes very acutely the characteristics of opinions as they are expressed in response to feelings or as the result of experience.[7] When an opinion is

---

[7] Trotter, W., "Instincts of the Herd in Peace and War." Published by T. Fisher Unwin, Ltd., London, 1916.

entertained with a feeling that it would be absurd, obviously unnecessary, unprofitable, undesirable, bad form, or wicked to inquire into it, then we know that the opinion in question is held instinctively and not as the result of individual experience. It is held because of its obviousness, which is another way of saying because it is dictated by the herd, that is, by the group of which the individual holding it forms a part. Opinions which are held as the result of experience do not offer such resistance to being inquired into. There is no such resistance to inquiry into the phenomena of physics and chemistry, the problems of mathematics, the proving of a geometrical theorem; but about matters of religion, morals, and politics it is largely in evidence. When, therefore, in wartime the individual regresses in his activities to lower ways of instinct expression he naturally also renounces the higher intellectual processes and drops to lower levels of emotional reaction to account for and to justify his conduct.

Another type of emotional reaction which equally has its roots in the unconscious is quite as common. I refer to the reaction of fear. From the category of qualities of the unconscious which I have cited it might appear that unconscious tendencies were all aggressive. The principle of the ambivalence of emotions, that for each feeling there is an exact opposite,[8] should have prepared us for the contrary. The feeling of fear has its origin in the necessity for change, for going forward into the region of the unknown, into situations which we no longer control, for parting with that feeling of omnipotence which belongs to the period of infancy. The infant, like the savage, has an exaggerated feeling of his own power and the omnipotence of his own thoughts. The savage tries to destroy the enemy by thoughts, that is, wishes, expressed in various magic ceremonies. The child wishes something, food; he cries, and presto! the food appears. This fancied control over things is not voluntarily given up, but only as a stern necessity, the result of the uncompromising invasion into this fairy-land of fancy of the cold, hard facts of reality. Not only is this world of phantasy not abandoned by the savage or the child, but it is never given up, and deep in the unconscious of man there always lurks that desire for omnipotence which we once knew when we still believed our thoughts brought things to pass, as they do nowadays in dreams, and for that feeling of safety we once knew as children when we were always able to flee from danger to the fostering care of a mother in whose ability to protect us we reposed absolute confidence.[9]

The desire for things as they always have been; this attachment to the past, the known, the familiar; the wish to continue in situations to which we have become fairly well adjusted and learned to control is the basis of reactionary and conservative policies of conduct, and it is when such relatively stable and familiar situations are destroyed and we are projected into situations with which we are no longer familiar and which we cannot control, in short into the unknown, that we react with fear. Fear, therefore, evidences our attachment to the past quite as truly as does hate.

Hate and fear are thus the two great type emotions that rise from the unconscious and take control of our conduct at times of regression. The characteristics of conduct motivated by hate I have already indicated. The conduct that comes from fear is primarily, of course, that group of actions to which we give the name of cowardice, and which is so severely censured by the herd in time of war because it is not useful to the group. There is a considerable group of persons, both within the military establishment and in civil life, who break down under the stresses of war conditions. They include many types of personality make-up, and the break manifests itself in all sorts of ways, from mild neuroses to frankly psychotic episodes. The consideration of this group constitutes a special chapter in psychopathology.

There is another aspect, however, of human conduct which war calls forth,

---

[8] See "Mechanisms of Character Formation."

[9] See "Mechanisms of Character Formation."

which is not to be described in such grim terms. War calls forth the loftiest type of aspirations, the most exalted acts of daring heroism and of self-sacrifice and unselfish devotion of which man is capable. This again might have been foreseen from the principle of ambivalency. What is the deeper meaning of this type of conduct?

As already indicated, the aims of the individual and the aims of the herd are of necessity frequently in opposition. The aims of the individual, as such, are essentially selfish, while the aims of the herd call for more or less reunuciation of selfishness and devotion to the good of the group, the larger whole, for conduct which is in essence unselfish. Thus it comes about that war picks up the problem of the herd. During periods of peace and prosperity individual aims come to be pronounced largely to the exclusion of social ones. They are in fact often emphasized to the point of evading social responsibilities of all sorts and looking upon the demands that grow out of such responsibilities as intrusions and invasions of personal rights and privileges. Such a state of affairs to the extent that it emphasizes selfishness and leads to a state of mind that courts the continuation of a stable state of society with no changes, or at best only a minimum of changes, is decidedly regressive. Life cannot go on and develop better conditions if it does not move forward into ever new regions that present new problems of adjustment. All these tendencies war peremptorily sweeps aside. The energies which were bound up in self-indulgence become available for national ends. Things are accomplished upon a prodigious scale and all manner of changes are brought to pass promptly and effectively, which would have been well-nigh impossible under the stagnant conditions of peace. Men are whipped by the new necessity into activity where energies had been lying dormant, and the whole nation takes on an aspect of activity quite different from its former one of quiescence and contentment. All of the multitudinous new activities have, too, this premium of social esteem, and so many a one whose life had been valueless and who had been wasting himself in useless dilettantism, is able to effect a social rehabilitation for himself, to reacquire a self-respect which had been lost because he had not the strength to overcome the numbing effect of too much ease. War has not only its destructive but its constructive aspect. Jones very well puts it when he says: [10] "War furnishes perhaps the most potent stimulus to human activity in all its aspects, good and bad, that has yet been discovered. It is a miniature of life in general at its sharpest pitch of intensity. It reveals all the latent potentialities of man, and carries humanity to the uttermost confines of the attainable, to the loftiest heights as well as to the lowest depths. It brings man a little closer to the realities of existence, destroying shams and remolding values. It forces him to discover what are the things that really matter in the end, what are the things for which he is willing to risk life itself. It can make life as a whole greater, richer, fuller, stronger and sometimes nobler. It braces a nation, as an individual, to put forth its utmost efforts, to the strange experience of bringing into action the whole energy of which it is capable.

"The results of this tremendous effort are what might have been expected. On the one side are feats of dauntless courage, of fearless heroism, of noble devotion and self-sacrifice, of incredible endurance, of instantaneous and penetrating apprehension, and of astounding intellectual achievement; feats which teach a man that he is greater than he knew. The other side need not be described in these days of horror. To appraise at their just value these two sides of war, to sound the depths as well as explain the heights, what is this other than to know the human mind?"

[10] Jones, Ernest, "War and Individual Psychology," *Sociological Review*, July, 1915.

Psychological Causes of War

CHAPTER V

FROM the consideration thus far given to the psychological aspects of the phenomenon of war, what can be said of its causes, not its political and economic causes, nor yet the causes that are put forth by the nations engaged in the conflict, but its psychological causes?

Already I have indicated what some of the causes might be. The fact that war to no small extent removes cultural repressions and allows the instincts to come to expression in full force is undoubtedly a considerable factor. In his unconscious man really takes pleasure in throwing aside restraints and permitting himself the luxury of the untrammeled expression of his primitive animal tendencies. The social conventions, the customs, forms, and institutions which he has built up in the path of his cultural progress represent so much energy in the service of repression. Repression represents continuous effort, while a state of war permits a relaxation of this effort and therefore relief.

We are familiar, in other fields, with the phenomena of the unconscious, instinctive tendencies breaking through the bounds imposed upon them by repression. The phenomena of crime and of so-called "insanity" represent such examples, while drunkenness is one instance familiar to all. *In vino veritas* expresses the state of the drunken man when his real, that is, his primitive self, frees itself from restraint and runs riot. The psychology of the crowd shows this mechanism at work particularly in such sinister instances as lynchings, while every crowd of college students marching, yelling and howling down the main street of the town after a successful cane rush exhibits the joy of unbottling the emotions in ways that no individual would for a moment think of availing himself of.

In addition to these active demonstrations of the unconscious there are those of a more passive sort. Not a few men are only too glad to step aside from the burden of responsibilities which they are forced to carry and seek refuge in a situation in which they no longer have to take the initiative, but must only do as they are directed by a superior authority. The government, in some of its agencies, takes over certain of their obligations, such as the support of wife and children, and they

clear out, free from the whole sordid problem of poverty, into a situation filled with dramatic interest. Then, too, if anything goes wrong at home they are not to blame, they have done their best, and what they have done meets with public approval. Is it any wonder that an inhabitant of the slums should be glad to exchange poverty and dirt, a sick wife and half starved children for glorious freedom, especially when he is urged by every sort of appeal to patriotism and duty to do so?

But all these are individual factors that enter into the causes of war. They represent some of the reasons why men like to fight, for it is difficult not to believe that if no one wanted to fight war would be possible at all. They too represent the darker side of the picture. War as already indicated offers, on the positive side, the greatest opportunities for the altruistic tendencies; it offers the most glorious occasion for service and returns for such acts the greatest possible premium in social esteem. But it seems to me that the causes of war lie much deeper, that they involve primarily the problems of the herd rather than the individual, and I think there are good biological analogies which make this highly probable.

I have already discussed the mechanism of integration and indicated how the development of the group as well as the organism was dependent upon the subordination of the parts to the whole. This process of integration tends to solve more and more effectively the problems of adjustment, particularly in some aspects, in the direction of ever-increasing stability. It is the process of the structuralization of function. This increase in stability, however, while it has the advantage of greater certainty of reaction, has the disadvantage of a lessened capacity for variation, and so is dependent for its efficiency upon a stable environment. As long as nothing unusual is asked of such a mechanism it works admirably, but as soon as the unusual arises it tends to break down completely. Life, however, is not stable; it is fluid, in a continuous state of flux, so while the development of structure to meet certain demands of adaptation is highly desirable and necessary, it of necessity has limits, which must sooner or later be reached in every instance. The most typical example of this is the process of growing old. The child is highly adjustable and for that reason not to be depended upon; the adult is more dependable but less adjustable; the old man has become stereotyped in his reactions. Nature's solution of this *impasse* is death. Death insures the continual removal of the no longer adjustable, and the places of those who die are filled by new material capable of the new demands. But it is the means that nature takes to secure the renewal of material still capable of adjustment that is of significance. From each adult, some time during the course of his life, nature provides that a small bit shall be detached which, in the higher animals, in union with a similar detached bit of another individual, will develop into a child and ultimately be ready to replace the adult when he becomes senile and dies. Life is thus maintained by a continuous stream of germ plasm and is not periodically interrupted in its course, as it seems to be, by death.

The characteristics of this detached bit of germ plasm are interesting. It does not manifest any of that complicated structure which we meet with in the other parts of the body. The several parts of the body are highly differentiated each for a specific function. Gland cells are developed to secrete, muscle cells to contract, bone cells to withstand mechanical stresses, etc. Manifestly development along any one of these lines would not produce an individual possessing, in its several parts, all of these qualities. Development has to go back of the point of origin of these several variations in order to include them all. In other words, regeneration has to start with relatively undifferentiated material. This is excellently illustrated by any of the lower, particularly the unicellular animals, in which reproduction is not yet sexual, but by the simple method of division. A cell comes to rest, divides into two, and each half then leads an independent existence. Before such a division and while the cell is quiescent, in the resting stage, as it is called, the differentiations of structure which it had acquired in its lifetime disappear, it becomes undifferentiated, relatively simple in structure. This process has been called dedifferentiation. When all the differentiations which had been acquired have been eliminated, then division—rejuvenescence—takes place.

From this point of view we may see in war the preliminary process of rejuvenescence. International adjustments and compromises are made until they can be made no longer; a condition is brought about which in Europe has been termed the balance of power, until the situation becomes so complicated that each new adjustment has such wide ramifications that it threatens the whole structure. Finally, as a result of the accumulated structure of diplomatic relations and precedents a situation arises to which adjustment, with the machinery which has been developed, is impossible and the whole house of cards collapses. The collapse is a process of dedifferentiation during which the old structures are destroyed, precedents are disavowed, new situations occur with bewildering rapidity for dealing with which there is no recognized machinery available. Society reverts from a state in which a high grade of individual initiative and development was possible to a relatively communistic and paternalistic state, the slate is wiped clear and a start can be made anew along lines of progress mapped out by the new conditions—rejuvenescence is possible.

War, from this point of view, is a precondition for development along new lines of necessity, and the dedifferentiation is the first stage of a constructive process. Old institutions have to be torn down before the bricks with which they were built can be made available for new structures. This accounts for the periodicity of war which thus is the outward and evident aspect of the progress of the life force which in human societies as elsewhere advances in cycles. It is only by such means that an *impasse* can be overcome.

War is an example of ambivalency on the grandest scale. That is, it is at once potent for the greatest good and the greatest evil: in the very midst of death it calls for the most intense living; in the face of the greatest renunciation it offers the greatest premium; for the maximum of freedom it demands the utmost giving of oneself; in order to live at one's best it demands the giving of life itself. "No man has reached his ethical majority who would not die if the real interests of the community could thus be furthered.

. . . . What would the world be without the values that have been bought at the price of death?" [11] In this sense the great creative force, love, and the supreme negation, death, become one. That the larger life of the race should go forward to greater things the smaller life of the individual must perish. In order that man shall be born again he must first die.

Does all this necessarily mean that war, from time to time, in the process of readjustment, is essential? I think no one can doubt that it has been necessary in the past. Whether it will be in the future depends upon whether some sublimated form of procedure can adequately be substituted: We have succeeded to a large extent in dealing with our combative instincts by developing sports and the competition of business, and we have largely sublimated our hate instinct in dealing with various forms of anti-social conduct as exhibited in the so-called "criminal." It remains to be seen whether nations can unite to a similar end and perhaps, by the establishment of an international court, and by other means, deal in a similar way with infractions of international law.

---

[11] G. Stanley Hall.

Some Tendencies Quickened by War

CHAPTER VI

TO WHAT ends are these elemental forces tending? No man can tell. It is the essence of life to produce the unexpected. The psychoanalyst reduces the instinctive trends of man to a very few, but what an endless variety results from their combinations, their differences of more or less, their compromises, distortions, and repressions! One is reminded of the few basic elements in the human face, and yet no two of the countless millions are alike! The pattern of the fine lines on the finger tips is different in every individual. The possibilities are practically infinite. And yet these tendencies are strong and seem to be pointing in certain general directions, and one may at least endeavor to pierce the future by means of speculation.

Democracy has been defined as a state of society in which "Every man is free to do that which he wills, provided he infringes not the equal freedom of any other man." [12] It would seem that social organization was tending in the direction of increased individual freedom, retaining and building up only such institutions as minister to the end of personal freedom by creating a *milieu* in which it can be safely exercised and brought to its fullest possible fruition. Combination, association in groups, is essential that each person may be secure to work out the best that is in him. The scholar, for example, the research scientist or the artist, could not exist in a primitive society all of the energies of which had to be focused upon the problem of obtaining food and protecting itself from enemies. Peace, industrialism, a reasonably stable structure built upon principles of law and order, specialized classes for producing the necessities, for defense and policing, are necessary that activities represented by science and art may be developed. In the world struggle now in progress those societies that are based upon the autocratic authority of some one man or class of men absolutely to control the destinies of the group and its individual members seem to be disintegrating, and the indications are clear that forces are at work that are attempting to give birth to a more clearly democratic form of government which will guarantee a greater measure of individual freedom. This would appear to be the big possibility that will ultimately come to pass, perhaps not immediately, but as a result of those forces which the war has stirred into action.

This fight for individual freedom is not new. It has been going on for ages and is exemplified every day in the conflict between parents and children. The family contains within itself elements that make for its ultimate disruption, as has been especially emphasized by psychoanalytic investigations. The basis of the conflict is the effort of the child to become emancipated from the control and protection of the home, so that ultimately he may be able to go forth into the world, free from such necessities, capable of standing upon his own feet, and in turn found a family of his own. This is the original form in which the conflict against constituted authority is cast and must mean, in the end, the overthrow of absolutism and the triumph of democracy, an end which will ultimately come to pass even if this present war should fail to accomplish it. Whether it shall be accomplished in whole or in part the results can hardly fail to effect progress in this general direction. There are many indications as to the specific lines along which this advance will take place.

Perhaps the most conspicuous advance in this direction, aside, of course, from the signs of a growing spirit of democracy in

---

[12] Herbert Spencer.

the European countries, is the movement for the emancipation of women. This movement can obviously no longer be stemmed by reactionary and conservative statesmen; it can be no more than delayed. The signs of the times are clear. Woman is coming rapidly to occupy a social and legal position that will be in every way on a footing of equality with the other sex. The war has hastened this movement as nothing else could, because it has demonstrated beyond argument that woman can do all the things that man can do and do them quite as well. The necessities of the warring nations have given her an opportunity to show her ability in almost every walk of life and she has stood the trial successfully.

Another movement in the same direction, not quite so obvious in its results, has been the taking over by the government of certain public utilities, in particular the railroads and the telegraph systems. This is but a part of that reaction against absolutism, that tends always to exploit the individual, that is directed against autocratic, capitalistic groups that grow up within a nation and which in their operation produce the same sort of hampering of the individual that monarchies do in larger measure.

As a part of this movement against the autocracy of capital there is developing an attitude towards large enterprises, which means that the employer of a large number of men has something further to look to than his balance sheets. He has a distinct social obligation, because it is after all the organized society of which he is a member that makes such enterprises possible, and he must give something back to society, in the form of service, for the privilege thus accorded to him. This means that he must look after the welfare of his employees, their health, and more particularly their working conditions. Work must be made as safe and wholesome as possible. Employers' liability acts, workmen's insurance, old-age pensions, factory sanitation, child labor laws, all point in that direction. We will probably see much more development along these lines, in particular a civil pension

act by the government and very probably a much more specific recognition of unions.

The possession of wealth itself is coming to mean something more than just having a lot of money. It is coming to imply social obligations in the way it is used. Society permits the existence of conditions which make the accumulation of wealth possible. It will soon undertake to say something about the way in which it can be used. Public displays of extravagance and wanton waste are long since taboo, while in the growing tax on income we see the beginning of a movement of repression which will ultimately result in an increased sense of the public obligations of great wealth. Money is but a symbol of power, of energy; and energy is of no value when it is idle. Taxes are one way in which the potential energy represented by money can be made kinetic; the money must be put to work, and when in addition the work that the money is put to is socially useful the significance of taxes, both for the public weal and also by bringing a measure of social esteem to the wealthy, is evident.

Another movement of similar significance is the taxing of inheritances. A social organism, like the individual, becomes senile and relatively defunct in proportion to the degree in which its ways of reacting become fixed, static; that is, in proportion to the degree in which its activities are controlled by its past and are unable to go forward in a relatively fluid, dynamic state in the process of adaptation to the ever-changing conditions which progress imposes. The laws of inheritance which permit persons to devise their property as they wish have been means whereby large accumulations of wealth have been kept intact, and controlled, no longer even by the living, but from the grave. It goes without saying that no human being is wise enough to look forward into the future, for a generation even, and say what will be the best way of using large powers, and any attempt to do so must, in general, lead to socially undesirable results. Inheritance taxes prevent the direction of large powers from being exercised by past generations; they tend to mobilize the energy to best meet present needs. Both of these economic tendencies, the taxing of incomes and inheritances, have been greatly accelerated by the necessities which this war has created.

These movements are but examples of a growing demand for an advanced, what has been called a "new democracy." The old slogan "all men are born equal" has had to be materially modified in the face of hard, incontrovertible facts. It was a manifest absurdity to claim that the born idiot was the equal of any other child. He suffers, as do all with congenital defects, from a handicap which can never be overcome. Some handicaps may be compromised with, as a missing limb, or actually be made an asset, as a grotesque deformity which the possessor may use as a means of livelihood. Some may even be overcome, as in the case of Demosthenes the stutterer, who became the greatest orator of Greece; but the mere statement of such differences implies inequality. And so the assumption that all men are born equal was modified to mean "equal before the law." Without dilating upon the manifest shortcomings of this formulation, for it is obvious that financial resources do exercise a modifying influence in the administration of the law, it is equally evident that this formulation falls short of our present ideals. Those ideals can now be better expressed by the phrase "equal opportunity" for all. This means that no man shall be deprived of a chance to attain success, and that, as a result, the constitution of a democracy shall be based upon merit rather than upon birthright or an accidental social position. The almost universal tendency to take public positions out of the control of political favoritism and make them subject to civil service requirements is the concrete expression of this attitude, imperfectly as this special mechanism may have functioned in particular instances. In all these senses not equality, but "inequality is of the essence of healthy social life," for manifestly some men are better equipped by natural advantages to do some things better than others. In a society in which merit gets its full recognition, each person would tend naturally to gravitate, as they do of course now, but in a less hampered way, to that position he could fill best, and thus his differences, the factors of inequality, would be utilized to the best advantage.

Another factor at work in this present war situation which makes for a democracy of equal opportunity has been a conscript army with promotions based upon service record. The consequent assembling of large numbers of men in camps without distinction of social class has undoubtedly had some tendency to break down these distinctions, a tendency which is undoubtedly further advanced when they come to share the hardships of actual service conditions at the front. A part of the mutual distrust of men in different walks of life is based upon their ignorance of each other. Living together, facing danger together, tends to wipe out such distrust built upon lack of acquaintance and respect, and helps to weld the individual members of the social group into a more sympathetic and understanding union. This same argument applies as well to men of different races, nationality, religious creeds, political persuasions, and in fact to all of the differences which ordinarily tend to split up society into smaller groups mutually ignorant of each other if not actually antagonistic.

Thus do we see the conditions of war giving opportunity for the expression of two diametrically opposed tendencies: the tendency to create the greatest possible opportunities for individual expression—individualism, and the tendency to subordinate individual energies to the service of the group—socialism.[13] This opposition represents the ambivalency of attitude towards the mutually opposed and opposite sides of the same fundamental problem.

---

[13] I have used the word socialism here not because it is perhaps an ideal word, but because it is as good as any other, inasmuch as all sorts of variations of theory are included under it and like terms which might have been used, such as collectivism and communism. In the sense here used it means only that necessary subordination of the individual to the group.

Individualism Versus Socialism—Love and Hate

CHAPTER VII

IT IS inconceivable that the great forces which have been set in motion by the war should become quiescent the moment peace is declared. They will proceed to operate if for no other reason than that of inertia. A great moving force of opinion, like a great body, cannot come to rest unless opposed by equal forces operating in the opposite direction. Then again this is no incidental war of conquest in which a nation of superior strength simply captures an inferior race a long distance from its base and reduces it to economic slavery. It is a world war in which fundamentally different principles, autocracy and democracy, are contending for the mastery.

As already indicated, the struggle for personal expression, individualism, begins in the home in the natural antagonism of parents and children, and has thus for its purpose the emancipation of the child. So, here, autocracy represents the relatively paternalistic type of government in which the monarch, representing, being symbolic of, the father, exercises a restraining and controlling direction of the individual, symbolic of the child, from which the individual is adways desiring to free himself. A democracy, in which the people choose their own ruler, approaches that eugenic ideal which has sometimes been facetiously expressed by saying that children should be able to choose their own parents. Already those who are looking into the future are recognizing the fact that the problems of the reconstruction period may be as large or larger than those of the war itself.

The contest will take on the form of a conflict between the two always-present tendencies which may be best formulated as socialism and individualism. Psychological conflicts take on the character of mutual antagonism between diametrically opposed tendencies, and it may be said of these two formulations, as of psychological conflicts in general, that both are right and both are wrong, for they only represent the two sides of the same issue—the issue of gaining the greatest expression. The group is fighting for the greatest opportunities for its expression, but in order to gain its goal it needs the highest development of its component members— the individuals that compose it. The individual is fighting for the greatest opportunities for his expression, but in order to gain his goal he needs the highest development of the group of which he is a member as a *milieu* in which, and only in which, he can bring to pass his personal ambitions.

Also, like all conflicts, a reaction which goes to either extreme is destructive. A complete reaction toward individualism with a consequent renouncing of all social ends would result in lawlessness and a state of comparative anarchy, which in the process of development would bring into power men untrained to the exercise of authority and unfitted by natural endowments to lead—the virtual substitution of a new autocracy of inefficiency. A complete reaction toward socialism with the renouncing of all individual aims would result in the establishment of a government which did not concern itself with the welfare of the individual units—an autocracy of power which would in turn array all individualistic tendencies against it. A compromise between the two extremes is necessary to get the maximum of benefit and the minimum of harm from each.

In ordinary times men divide themselves into two camps variously named, conservatives and progressives for instance, which represent these two tendencies, and out of the clash of these opposing factions a generally useful compromise results. In times of revolution the reaction is wont to go to extremes and produce a state of affairs from which it takes a long time to settle down to a workable middle ground. Then is the psychological moment for great constructive leadership that is wise enough to hold the masses together with some constructive policy while taking advantage of the fluidity of the situation to bring to pass such radical reforms as will preserve, as a permanent gain, as many of the possibilities as have been inherent in the period of readjustment and which represent real progress. This is work for those men of genius which such times, sooner or later, call forth. If, however, the process of de-differentiation goes beyond a certain point it would seem as if it had to complete itself, so to speak, before reconstruction can begin.

The most difficult and the most immediate problem that confronts a victorious nation is its treatment of its defeated foe. This is made especially difficult, because it must come after a period during which every effort has been made to weld together each party to the conflict in a united front against the enemy, and the methods that are used for this purpose are the methods dictated by hate. The banality of the appeal to popular sentiment; the reiteration and emphasis laid upon unsupported statements and upon plain, evident wishes, demonstrates that the moving forces that unite the group are emotional and largely regressive. The appeal to patriotism, of course, as already implied, has its distinct constructive and progressive aspects. Reason, at least so far as it is called upon at all, especially in the early stages of a conflict, is confined to finding arguments with which to support the emotional attitude—the mechanism known as rationalization. This mechanism is well in evidence in the effort usually made by both parties to the conflict to show that the war was started by the enemy, whose attitude was purely offensive, while for themselves it was as purely defensive. Similarly, each side, by the same mechanism of rationalization, supports a claim to the inherent righteousness of their cause and the unrighteous-

ness of the cause of the enemy.[14] This is the fluid, emotionally laden situation into which a truly great leader may project himself and, gathering up all the loose ends of reason and feeling alike, formulate the whole movement in terms that cement, direct, and lead popular thinking. It is the great opportunity, too, for turning the enormous energies of the herd into channels which shall effect constructive ends, for utilizing the free energies for the larger purposes by detaching them from their several purely selfish attempts at realization and directing them, through the medium of some symbol such as "making the world safe for democracy," into activities which shall be of service in the largest sense.

Hate, pure and simple, is always destructive in its tendencies. It can be used constructively only indirectly, by being directed against persons, institutions, ways of thinking which it is necessary to clear away in order to substitute something better. A new building cannot be constructed out of the bricks of an old one without first tearing down the old structure. The utilization of hate in this way makes it serve creative ends. The danger is, of course, in failing to keep it in leash.

It is just this danger of hate overstepping the necessary limits of its constructive task that makes the reconstruction period so full of difficulties. Each war contains the material for the next war in the excessive advantages which the conqueror takes by imposing humiliations upon the conquered, as, for example, in depriving him of territory. The latter is the typical example which stands as a menace to the resumption of friendly relations. It is felt as an injustice, and the day is looked forward to when the wrong can be righted, the lost possessions re-

---

[14] Perhaps no better material offers for the study of these mechanisms than the stories circulated in times of war of the atrocities committed by the enemy. Of course atrocities are committed, and many of the stories are true or founded in truth, but equally many of them are made of whole cloth and represent projected wishes of what the author of the stories would like to do and like to believe true in order to justify his hate and retaliatory measures based upon it. See in this connection Jung, C. G., "Collected Papers on Analytical Psychology," chap. IV, "A Contribution to the Psychology of Rumor." Published by Moffat, Yard & Co., New York, 1917.

gained, and too, some additional territory taken besides to redress the humiliation suffered. The formulation of peace terms, therefore, taxes the ingenuity of the greatest minds to effect an adjustment that will be lasting.

Until recently, to be sure with notable exceptions, there has been no thought of a lasting peace between nations. International relations were always strained and armed force was trusted as the only efficient argument. Now, on the contrary, the air is filled with speculations on the possibility of a more stable basis for international relations which will make war, if not impossible, at least less easily possible. Some psychological speculations regarding the principles involved may not be out of place. As previously indicated, reactions of nations as well as individuals may be classified on the basis of their relative maturity or immaturity from the developmental point of view, and the criteria for such a judgment rest in the extent to which the reactions show that instinct is directed and controlled by reason, and also in the degree of the integration shown by the breadth or height of the highest aims. The former criterion needs no further comment; the latter will bear some further explanation. In the primitive manifestations of life the larger good is the welfare of the cell only; other cells receive no consideration. In a somewhat more advanced stage of multicellularity in which the organism is represented by a loosely associated group of cells, the larger good compasses the group, and so on. So with primitive man, he is largely selfish, but the larger good as he knows it includes the group of which he is a member —often nothing more than a small wandering tribe. Later in the history of development the tribes are larger and may even be united in groups of tribes or nations, and as there is this progressive increase in size and complexity with corresponding integration the larger good comes progressively to apply to the larger and more heterogeneous association. So nations come to be held together by the common purposes of the individuals composing them, but at the same time to exist in a constant state of antagonism, if not

actual warfare, with other nations. This conflict comes to be in part expressed, among civilized nations, in their diplomatic maneuvers for advantage, and in an established economic and industrial rivalry. It tends to be maintained, in no small part, by the lack of acquaintance with each other maintained by differences of language, religion, and customs and by natural geographical barriers such as mountain ranges, rivers, and oceans, and by distance in general, both of which tend only slowly to give way to improved means of intercommunication. The inhabitants of neighboring countries may thus come to be looked upon not only as aliens, but as natural enemies, only waiting the opportunity to seize some advantage of conquest and from whom they must be prepared at all times to defend themselves. Like the wild animals of the jungle they know no friends except those of their own kind. The question now is, whether, in view of the wide prevalence of the interest in a permanent peace there are possibilities of developing an integration at a higher level than a national level, namely, at an international level.

On the face of it, it would seem, in fact it must be, that the nations of the world are more favorably circumstanced for an attempt of this sort than ever before. The enormous development of international trade relations, the correspondingly great improvement of transportation facilities, the increase in the travel between countries that lie wide apart, the substitution of the teaching of the dead languages by the modern languages in our schools and universities, the study of the histories, development, science, literature, and art of foreign countries, have brought us into far closer contact with our contemporaries all over the world than ever before, and must have had a considerable effect in wiping out that feeling of mystery about other peoples which makes us feel them as alien and tends to keep alive a spirit of distrust, fear, and hate. While the study of such sciences as anthropology, ethnology, comparative philology, and psychology have taught us that in reality all men are kin. Whether or not the present time is ripe for such a wider expansion of human interests as is implied in a "league of nations" remains to be seen, but at least to try to effect such an adjustment as is implied in an effort to bring the great nations of the earth to a common understanding is not only a move in the right direction, but, even if it fails to accomplish all that its most ardent advocates wish, it cannot fail—because it is rightly directed—to bring the goal nearer, to speed the day of its actual accomplishment. It may be hoped that if all nations cannot get together in a league of nations, at least some of them can, and that future problems will be on the higher plane of integrating such groups.

To the end of helping to bring to pass higher international relations certain attitudes of mind must be modified as they relate to the international situation. To put it briefly, the indulgences of hate must be curbed. Hate, it must be understood, can serve creative ends only when it tears down to make possible better building. If it exceeds this limit it becomes unconditionally destructive, and, it is worth while to contemplate, far more destructive to those who indulge in it than to those upon whom its force is expended. Hate makes little men and stands an everlasting barrier to the development of a broad, deep, well-rounded character.

In a war such as the present one, for example, force has to be used. The enemy that would destroy must be made impotent for harm; our own physical integrity must be preserved if we are to be in a position to exercise our powers for the larger ends. But force, so far as possible, needs to be limited to such utilitarian purposes, it needs to be used with a clear vision to effect certain well-defined purposes, and those purposes should compass large, constructive ends that will benefit us primarily perhaps but surely will minister to the wider purpose. If this be effected we will in the end benefit far more by the results that will accrue to us indirectly than if we had kept in mind solely selfish aims. The desire, therefore, to make our enemy suffer, just for the purpose of gaining satisfaction from his sufferings, must be put aside once and

for all as either a worthy or a valuable object of war.

I am minded at this point to refer again to the analogy, based upon the destruction wrought, between reactions that are relatively mature or immature. The analogy is to the history of the treatment of children. Without going into details I may say that perhaps no page of history is blacker, none testifies to more helpless suffering, none shows man so unreservedly at his worst. Children have been treated as chattels, the innocent objects of hate in all its gruesome forms; they have been enslaved, deprived of comfort, made the objects of every cupidity, maimed and beaten, subjected to every indignity and abuse, killed. Through it all there must have run a golden thread of love, but it was stretched almost to the breaking point many a time. Only lately have we learned, in a practical way, that love, not hate, is the open sesame to the child's character. Only through love do children come to blossom forth into good and useful personalities that hate served only to warp and deform. Love must be the basis upon which any lasting good can be built; hate only serves to cripple and retard. The same lesson has been learned, or, more correctly, is being learned, in the treatment of infantile types of reaction as we see them in the so-called insane, criminal, and defective classes generally. Kindness has stricken off chains that cruelty and punishment have ever served to make the heavier. While repression is a necessary factor in education, it can never alone produce the best results, and even then it must be imposed by love and only with the desire of creating the most favorable conditions of development by making the best way at once the easier and the most desirable way.

As I have indicated, reactions of hate always testify to a primitiveness in the repressive process. Hate is the method of repression before an instinct can be sublimated so as not to require it. The relatively inefficient artisan may hate his competitor who is more skillful, and perhaps entertains desires to exert physical violence against him. His children, who have had larger opportunities for development, may have learned that the best way to overcome a competitor is to do better work than he does, and if they are capable of it hate is no longer an emotion of which they feel the need. We may fear and hate a person whose opinions differ from ours until we learn to know him and realize that he is made of the same stuff as ourselves, and is really striving for better things as we are—perhaps for the same ends by only a slightly modified method. The clashing of instincts gives way to the meeting of minds. When men can realize that they all are after the same things, that growth is in the same general direction for all, they will come to realize that they can better effect their several purposes by pooling their interests than by insisting too strongly upon individual recognition. Devotion to selfish ends makes enemies, consecration to service invariably commands a following. "Everywhere, we learn only from those whom we love." [15]

If, therefore, it be true that autocracies, absolute monarchies based upon the fiction of divine authority, represent relatively immature forms of government, we can expect to change the spirit of people who live under them only by bringing them to our point of view. Ultimately this can be done only by bringing them to see that our way of seeing is the better, and they will come to agree with us only if they learn to respect us. Respect must be mutual and based upon mutual understanding, which amounts to saying that hate cannot bring it about, but only love. A system of exploitation of a conquered foe, a continuing repression with reprisals and all the machinery of modern society turned to the uses of revenge cannot bring such a state to pass. It is not the way we would treat an erring child, nor should it be the way we should treat a beaten foe, whose error has been that he was actuated by standards of conduct we believe to be lower—less matured—than our own. If our cause is as holy as we are pleased to think it, if the enemy is as primitive as we are pleased to claim, then we have the

golden opportunity to show our superiority after we have beaten him. If we do not do it, then he still has the right to think that our alleged convictions were but pronounced with the lips, that they did not issue from the heart. There must be a "victory of justice" rather than a "victory of power" if those instinctive tendencies of hate are to be stilled in the hearts of our erstwhile enemy and justice "must involve no distinction between those to whom we wish to be just and those to whom we do not wish to be just." [16]

I know the difficulties of proceeding along the lines indicated, but the path of hate has been pursued since the world began, and wars have followed wars. No harm can come from trying some new way, and when that way is the way Christianity has always taught, those who have a profound respect for the wisdom of the folk soul may well be inclined to follow. The difficulties of making a basis of peace satisfactory to all of the multitude of interests involved are stupendous, as are the obstacles to be overcome in establishing a league of nations that will function. Of such matter I am not competent to speak. I can only call attention to certain psychological factors involved. In any event, the United States occupies a position of supreme importance and incalculable possibilities in the council of nations, and I believe that the amount of force she will be able to bring to bear for good will depend upon the possibility of putting aside issues of selfishness and hate. It will need a clear vision and great faith to see the way and follow it.

The very clear principle involved is that reprisals, or other punitive measures, are useful when addressed to constructive ends. Speaking in physiological terms, they are useful for conditioning behavior along desirable lines after the manner of the conditioned reflex. When used solely for selfish purposes, as a means of self-indulgence in hate and self-exploitation, they can only be expected to be destructive in their final results.

---

[15] Goethe.

[16] President Wilson.

The Socially Handicapped

CHAPTER VIII

NO MAN can say just what will be the great problems after the war. We can only see in a general way what must grow out of present conditions, for it is of the nature of life to grow as it advances, and questions will arise which could not have been predicted; but I will follow along one of the problems in accordance with the principles already laid down to show where it may lead. I refer to the problem of the crippled soldier.

To be crippled nowadays is to be disgraced. The loss of an arm or a hand so often means drunkenness the night before the accident, or lack of skill, or mental dullness, and anyway it makes the man inferior to his fellows if he was not before. He cannot get a job as easily if at all, and then only at some unskilled work or as a mark of charity. The industrial cripple is a marked man, literally, and tries to hide his defect. An employers' liability act which fixes the loss of an eye at a given sum and makes total blindness a much larger burden for the employer to bear, makes that same employer chary of hiring men already blind of one eye for fear the loss of the other will subject him to compensation at the rate for total blindness.

The war, temporarily at least, makes a mutilation a badge of honor. The man who has lost an arm in the defense of his country is a hero and is proud of his loss. In his pride it compensates him for his loss, and perhaps may be a means of bridging the gap to the industrial cripple. With so many obviously crippled men to provide for there has come as a stimulus to manufacturers that fine fire of enthusiasm to help the boys who have sacrificed so much by inventing means whereby they may operate the ordinary machines of industrial life efficiently. With the problem of labor which will arise after the war, when foreign countries will need their own for the rebuilding of their home countries, the cripple may find that the way has been provided for his social rehabilitation. Such a state of affairs may well lead to a revaluation of the cripple, a realization of his usefulness and an effort to make his possibilities available which will result, not only in a modified attitude towards him, with the necessary changes in law and custom, but may easily affect society's attitude to all of its less efficient members all along the line.

For every man, no matter how limited in mind or body, there is something that he can do that is worth while that he should do. Few can be 100 per cent efficient, but few need to be wholly lacking in usefulness. The limited-service class of the Army represents an acknowledgment of this principle, which should really make for a still broader viewpoint and govern our relations with all, including those classes now grouped under such misleading terms as criminal, defective, insane.[17]

Parents do not abandon their children because they are not as smart as their neighbor's children. Society should do as much and in the same spirit. Not only is such an attitude useful to society, but the cripple, the defective, is entitled to be considered in this way. Socialism is trying, by methods of taxation among other means, to abolish that state of helpless poverty of so many that effectually destroys all ambition, all hope. Poverty of mind and body is deserving of as much consideration if the "equality" of democracy means equal opportunity. Everyone is entitled to a chance to use that which he has; it should be the object of social organization to see that he gets it. The type of young man who has been injured by wounds represents the flower of our

[17] See "Principles of Mental Hygiene."

[27]

manhood, and it would not only be unjust but it would be a ruinous principle from every point of view if he were relegated, even in his own feelings, to a state of uselessness.

Just as in the smaller groups within the nations, it is but justice to treat the less efficient, less mature individuals after this manner, so in a group of nations the same principle should hold. A league of nations may include some one that is not culturally in as advanced a state of development as the others. Such a nation should be given a chance to develop, and repressive measures, like the punishment of children, should never be resorted to just to indulge hate, but only to make the way of development the easier way.

Such statements as these, I know, especially when I speak in terms of international affairs, sound visionary, but I am using such illustrations to point a principle that I believe is true. Actual conditions may make the application of the principle impossible, but they cannot destroy the value of keeping it in mind.

If this war makes at all for constructive ends, those ends will be the granting of a larger measure of opportunity to all the handicapped peoples of the earth—the unfortunate among us, crippled in mind or body, or by industrial and economic repressions or by racial, religious, or political prejudices, and a like opportunity extended as between nations. Civilization, which has been so taxed by the release of the primitive instincts in an orgy of destruction, has—by the very clearing away of standards which had survived their period of usefulness and became static and therefore barriers to further progress—an unparalleled opportunity to rise to greater heights on the path to higher integrations, greater possibilities of coordinated action for the common good of all.

In the life of individuals it often happens that a great misfortune is the turning point in their careers and, bravely met, may turn out to have been a great beneficence. Unfortunately misfortune does not always result in this way. Wars in the past have often produced only suffering, but such an end may not be the only possible one. Has the time come when the greatest of all national calamities can be made the greatest of all national opportunities? Is there a developed, constructive statesmanship equal to turning the tide towards the great constructive possibilities? The Allied nations are in a position to answer these questions. They stand on the threshold of the greatest of all opportunities.